NATIONAL GEOGRAPHIC

School Publishing

T0306545

Communities

Jason Harte

PICTURE CREDITS

Cover, 9 (below), 10, 11 (above), 13 (below left), 14 (right), Getty Images; 1, 4 (all),
5 (left), 7 (all), 8 (all), 11 (left), 14 (below left & above left), 16 (above right, center
right, below left & below right), Photolibrary.com; 2, 6, 16 (above left), APL/Corbis;
5 (right), 11 (below right), Michael Newman/PhotoEdit, Inc.; 9 (above), 12, 16 (center left),
Bill Aron/PhotoEdit, Inc.; 13 (above right), Mary Kate Denny/PhotoEdit, Inc.; 15 (above),
Steve Skjold/PhotoEdit, Inc.; 15 (below) Jeff Greenburg/PhotoEdit, Inc.

Produced through the worldwide resources of the National Geographic Society,
John M. Fahey, Jr., President and Chief Executive Officer; Gilbert M. Grosvenor,
Chairman of the Board; Nina D. Hoffman, Executive Vice President and President,
Books and Education Publishing Group.

PREPARED BY NATIONAL GEOGRAPHIC SCHOOL PUBLISHING

Ericka Markman, Senior Vice President and President Children's Books and Education
Publishing Group; Steve Mico, Senior Vice President and Publisher; Marianne Hiland,
Editorial Director; Lynnette Brent, Executive Editor; Michael Murphy and Barbara Wood,
Senior Editors; Bea Jackson, Design Director; David Dumo, Art Director; Margaret
Sidlowsky, Illustrations Director; Matt Wascavage, Manager of Publishing Services;
Sean Philpotts, Production Manager.

MANUFACTURING AND QUALITY MANAGEMENT

Christopher A. Liedel, Chief Financial Officer; Phillip L. Schlosser, Director;
Clifton M. Brown III, Manager.

BOOK DEVELOPMENT

Ibis for Kids Australia Pty Limited.

Copyright © 2006 National Geographic Society. All rights reserved. Reproduction of the
whole or any part of the contents without written permission from the publisher is
prohibited. National Geographic, National Geographic *Windows on Literacy*, and the
Yellow Border are registered trademarks of the National Geographic Society.

Published by the National Geographic Society
1145 17th Street, N.W.
Washington, D.C. 20036-4688

ISBN: 0-7922-6065-1

Fourth Printing 2018
Printed in the USA

Contents

playing

working

helping

People live in communities.
Talk about what these people are doing.

shopping

learning

Different Communities

People live in many different kinds of communities.

Some people live in big cities.

Some people live in suburbs.

Some people live in small towns.

Jobs in a Community

There are many jobs in a community. People who do these jobs help the community.

A police officer helps people stay safe.

A teacher helps students learn.

A librarian helps check out books.

A crossing guard helps people cross the road.

9

What Do People Need?

People need many different things. People can find these things in their community.

People need a place to live.

People need food.

People need clothes.

People need friends!

11

What Do People Want?

People want many different things. People can find these things in their community.

People want to see movies.

People want to buy ice cream.

People want to buy bicycles.

baseball field

farmers' market

playground

14

Talk about these places in Angela's community. Talk about places in your community.

school

shopping mall

community

help

job

live

need

people

want

work

Picture Glossary

city

crossing guard

librarian

police officer

teacher

town